BEHIND THE SCREENS

HOW THE INTERNET WORKS & HOW TO MAKE IT WORK FOR YOU

NIRAJ LAL

ILLUSTRATED BY AŚKA

For Ash, Ella and Miles, and for Dad —NNL

First published 2026 by University of Queensland Press
PO Box 6042, St Lucia, Queensland 4067 Australia

University of Queensland Press (UQP) acknowledges the Traditional Owners and their custodianship of the lands on which UQP operates. We pay our respects to their Ancestors and their descendants, who continue cultural and spiritual connections to Country. We recognise their valuable contributions to Australian and global society.

uqp.com.au
reception@uqp.com.au

Cover, internal illustrations and contributor illustrations by Aśka
Typeset in Mohr by University of Queensland Press
Printed in China by 1010 Printing International

University of Queensland Press is supported by the Queensland Government through Arts Queensland.

University of Queensland Press is assisted by the Australian Government through Creative Australia, its principal arts investment and advisory body.

A catalogue record for this book is available from the National Library of Australia.

ISBN 978 0 7022 6894 6 (pbk)
ISBN 978 0 7022 7044 4 (epdf)
ISBN 978 0 7022 7045 1 (epub)

University of Queensland Press uses papers that are natural, renewable and recyclable products made from wood grown in well-managed forests and other controlled sources. The logging and manufacturing processes conform to the environmental regulations of the country of origin.

CONTENTS

WELCOME TO THE INTERNET

Hello! I'm **Nij**, a scientist and writer living in Melbourne where I host the ABC's *Imagine This* kids' podcast.

The internet is **absolutely incredible**. FaceTime someone in Tanzania? No worries. Learn how to build a chicken coop? Here's an AI-generated summary with a step-by-step video. What's your cousin up to? Here are ten photos!

But, despite how **amazing** it is – and useful and informative and social and hilarious and **life-changing** – I wrote this book because the internet isn't *always* what it seems. Things are happening **behind the screens** that change what we *see* to try to change what we *do*: what we buy, what we believe and how long we stay online.

And they're actually really effective. The internet is **changing us**! The average Australian now spends 2.5 hours a day on their phone – and 17 years over a lifetime looking at a screen connected to the internet. We can't get enough.

Whether or not you're online a lot already, you're probably going to be using the internet, AI and other online technologies **more and more** in years to come, so it's helpful to explore how those technologies are **using you** a little too.

Politicians and scientists talk about this stuff all the time, but not always *with* young people – the ones inheriting the internet and **a world shaped by it**. My aim with this book is to help change that. I don't work for the government or for any tech companies, and I'm not trying to sell you anything. But I do think that if you get **real info** on how things actually work, you'll be empowered to make decisions in your own best interests.

This book is a guide to what goes on behind the screens. Its purpose is to shine some light on how the internet works, help you to be eSafe and social, figure out what is fact and what is fiction, interact with AI, look after your data privacy, and more. Basically, this book is designed to help you **be more aware** about what's going on online and why – and what that means **for you**.

It doesn't replace what you're getting taught in school (your teachers *should* have that under control) or tell you how to find the best content (google it! [jks]). It also doesn't aim to give you an intro for everything on the internet (it currently contains more than 150 trillion GB of data – and growing every day ...). But it will arm you with some info to help you be online in the **best** way possible.

Let's go!

chapter 1

HOW THE INTERNET WORKS

If you type a website address (like **google.com** or **behindthescreens.me**) into a **browser** (like Chrome or Safari or Firefox) and hit 'enter', *amazing* things happen.

What you type into your browser is sent out from your device through **wifi radio waves**. Here's an example:

IP-address 60.240.19.205 wants data from www.behindthescreens.me; here are their phone details; please send through the data ...

The router on the wall **sends this message** as light through NBN optic fibres outside your house to your internet service provider. They ask, 'Have you paid your bill?' and, 'Are you allowed to access this website?' and then send the message on to a **domain name server** (which is like a national internet post office).

'You can get unlimited information about anything on the internet, and there are videos that can teach you whatever you want to know.'
ARLO, 10

The domain name server finds where the end website's information is located (say, a data centre in the UK) and sends the message out via **undersea cables** to the exact address, which then sends the website's info back out to your device.

All this takes about 100 milliseconds, quicker than the blink of an eye! *Amazing*.

This process can transmit messages, emails, photos, videos, games – **anything at all** that you can see on the internet. It's incredibly fast, pretty reliable and one of the most life-changing inventions of human history.

We call the information that's being sent out **data**.

WHAT IS DATA?

Data is just a word for **organised information**. People have recognised the value of organising, saving and sharing data for as long as we've been around – it's just been done through songs and stories instead of hard drives. But, with the internet, the amount of data we are generating and transmitting is so, so much greater.

Alongside the 'useful' data being sent – the website or text or video – **other information** is being transmitted too. This other information is called **metadata**.

WHAT IS METADATA?

Metadata is information **about the content**, not the content itself.

Take the example of a WhatsApp message. The data is what you actually write (maybe: 'Hey, let's go to the park after school'). The metadata includes the **other information** that you transmit along with the message. This includes your phone's make and model and IP address (like an internet name for your device), plus a whole lot more about the message, such as:

- **when** you wrote it
- **who** you sent it to
- **where** you were when you sent it
- **how long** you took to write it
- **how many times** you erased it and rewrote it
- **when** the person you sent it to read it
- **where** they were when they read it
- **how long** they read it for ...

WhatsApp messages are **encrypted end-to-end**. WhatsApp says they can't access those messages. But they can and do **access the metadata**, save it and share it between all of the companies owned by the same group of people (Instagram, Facebook, Oculus etc.), who then use this information in lots of other ways.

Cookies count as metadata too. When websites ask if they can store cookies on your device, they're saving **small files**. These contain information like passwords, previous browsing histories and purchasing records. Websites use them to remember your information and tailor themselves just for you.

This is different to a **cache**, which is your browser's **temporary storage** of files, webpages, images and similar to make things load faster.

Nearly everything you do on the internet is tracked and recorded through metadata for the simple reason that it is **valuable**!

It's actually what **pays** for much of the internet.

chapter 2

FREE-DOM!

The internet is a place of **incredible freedom** – where you can go almost anywhere you want, learn almost anything you'd like and see almost anything at all.

You can connect with people, share information, see how others respond and explore who you want to be. It's absolutely **revolutionary**.

And often we can do all this for **free**! We don't pay a cent to use YouTube, TikTok, Snapchat, Instagram, Facebook, Google, WhatsApp, Threads, Messenger and the list goes on ...

But the funny thing is that these tech companies are some of the *richest* in the world. If they're free, how do they make **so much money**?

The simple answer is that other companies pay *lots* of money to **show you ads** while you're using various platforms, services and apps.

ADVERTISERS AND DATA

In the past, companies paid money to **advertise** their products on highway billboards, in television commercials, and in newspapers and magazines, all in the hope that a potential customer *might* see it.

And it was the same with the early internet. The first search engines, AltaVista and Yahoo, had landing pages *crammed* with ads for things you'd never buy in a million years. But in 1998, two uni students figured out a new way to **target ads to users** based on their search data *and their metadata*. They offered this targeted service to advertisers through their new company, and advertisers **paid them lots** to use it. That company was Google, and it changed the internet forever.

Now, instead of paying for a huge billboard on a highway, or a big ad in a newspaper, companies can **target their ads** specifically to the people *most likely* to buy their product.

Have you ever seen an ad showing you something that you've *just* been talking about? Or something specific that you're *actually* interested in? This isn't a coincidence. It's because, somewhere on the internet (actually, in many different places), there's a **super detailed profile** about who you are, where you go, who your friends are, who you're influenced by and pretty much *everything* you're interested in – all based on **your data and metadata**.

If this sounds spooky, that's okay – it is!

what do advertisers pay for?

People who want to advertise their products through Google (the biggest internet ad company) pay for **impressions** (when you see their ad – Google keeps a tally) or **click-throughs** (when you click on a link in the ad). Typical prices range from $1 to $2 per *thousand* impressions and from $1 to $50 per click-through.

It works by advertisers telling Google **how much** they want to spend on advertising and **what kind of person** they want to target. Google then matches this with all the information they have about you – like your location, what you've searched for in the past, what you're searching for now, how likely it is that you might buy a certain product and heaps of other things – to show you stuff that you might want to click on, so they can **get paid**.

Google loves it! And companies love it too! Almost all the websites that show ads (about half of the websites on the entire internet) use Google Ads. It's **incredibly successful**. Google makes hundreds of billions of dollars every year through ads.

building a profile

The curious thing is that your information doesn't affect only the ads *you* see – but also the ads seen by **anyone like you**.

How does that work? By using your information and what they have learnt about you, they build a **marketing profile** of who you are and how you act.

'My dad was just talking about buying a paddleboard, when all of a sudden he started to get all these ads about paddleboards.'
ELISE, 11

Then, when anyone displays similar traits or acts in similar ways (for example, follows a particular singer or clicks on an ad for skate shoes) they can put you into a **similar marketing category**.

And *then*, they can use the behaviour of everyone in that category to **predict one another's behaviour**, meaning they can show them the specific ads that will get the most clicks and make the most money. The same goes for every single person on the internet.

This means that when you go online, in addition to watching content or messaging or being on socials, you're also providing companies with **free research** on what other people like you like to do, and they use this info to make money from advertisers.

being a product

Receiving targeted information can be **really useful**. If Google knows where you live and you search for bike tools, it can suggest stores nearby. If you listen to a certain song on Spotify a lot, it can suggest other songs that you might like. If you're starting to get interested in playing guitar, it can be helpful to see good content about it.

But it's worth remembering that **even free things come at a cost**. If you're not paying for a product, chances are you *are* the product! And maybe the biggest consequence of that is how the internet is changing our behaviour.

surveillance capitalism and the attention economy

With your marketability to internet companies like Google being based on how much they know about you, there is an incentive for those companies to know **as much as possible** about you. And because how many ads you see is based on how long you spend on a website, there is an incentive for ad-showing websites or apps to **keep you engaged** for as long as possible.

All this together means that, as we find ourselves rocketing through the 21st century, companies are competing furiously to:

- learn as much as possible about us to make money by selling that information to other companies (sometimes known as **surveillance capitalism**)
- keep us engaged with their websites for as long as possible so they can show more ads (sometimes called the **attention economy**).

What will this mean as companies get better and better at doing these two things? Can we find something truly new if we're only shown stuff based on our past interests? What might it mean for our privacy, our attention, our communities and our planet?

And **what can we do** about it?

chapter 3

WHERE'S MY PHONE?!

Look at any adult close to you and notice how long it takes for them to pick up their phone. You shouldn't have to wait too long. The average Australian checks their phone 85 times a day – about every 11 minutes during waking hours. Adults in the Western world *touch* them on average **more than 2000 times a day**.

Most adults can't remember the last time they went 24 hours without a phone. They feel **anxious** leaving home without them, and they **worry** if it's got less than 20% battery or they're heading out of reception. And it's not just adults – it's anyone who owns a phone, **kids included**.

Checking our phones is often **the first thing** we do in the morning and **the last thing** we do at night. Any possible moment we get alone is another opportunity.

Toilet break? Check. Waiting for the bus? Check. Standing in a queue? Check. **We're obsessed!**

Interestingly, people usually have **some kind of routine** when they pick up their phone. Depending on their age, that could look something like this:

> *Check WhatsApp; check Instagram, scroll for a little while; check the news; check TikTok, get lost in a rabbit hole; check messages; check the news, scroll for a bit; check WhatsApp again, realise they've already checked it; slowly re-emerge into the physical world wondering what they were doing on their phone ...*

'Getting a phone felt like the beginning of a new chapter of your life a bit.'
MADDY, 13

And the *wild* thing is this: they'll probably do exactly the same thing in a few minutes' time! **But why?**

GUIDELINES

The Australian Government's current screen time recommendation for children and young adults aged 5–17 is: 'no more than 2 hours of sedentary recreational screen time per day. This does not include screen time needed for schoolwork.'

THE SCIENCE OF DOPAMINE

The science of why we love to check our phones is well-known. Around 600 million years ago, an ancient worm that was the common ancestor of jellyfish, sea anemones, and you and me, found a way to make a chemical called **dopamine**, which made it feel good after eating a nice meal.

"(HO HO NH_2)"

The worm liked this feeling so much it tried to find another nice meal and then another. All these nice meals helped the worm grow strong and pass on its dopamine-making genes to the next generation of worm kids – and nearly every animal on the planet has been on the hunt for dopamine ever since!

Dopamine is released when humans are **'rewarded'** with something too. Eating sweet foods, finding ten bucks on the ground, receiving a nice message or getting a 'like' on social media all **trigger** the release of dopamine in our brains – which feels great. This process is known as a **reward pathway**. (Other chemicals are involved, but dopamine is one of the most important.)

What's funny is that dopamine is also released just by **thinking** we might get a reward. Just *looking* at a dessert menu, *checking* your feed or *asking* to have a sleepover at a friend's place will release dopamine too.

'There's no way I can talk to my older brother when he's on his phone. It's like he's in a different world.'
LAURENCE, 11

The happy dings of new messages arriving, the little love hearts and smiley face reacts, the likes and follows, the pretty photos and funny videos, the small acts of validation of who we are: they all give us **hits of dopamine** – all day, every day, 365 days a year. Another thing is, with repeated exposure over time, we **need more** of an activity to feel the same buzz that we felt the first time round. And, while dopamine can help us feel pleasure, its absence can feel like pain.

The story gets more interesting too. In tests in the 1930s and 1940s, scientists found that when rats were trained to receive a reward by pressing a button, if the reward came *unpredictably*, they ended up **compulsively** pressing the button – just like adults check their phones.

People now check their phones so much that they've been described as pacifiers. Just like a baby sucks on a dummy to be soothed, people reflexively check their phones **for the same relief**.

Whether or not **phone addiction** or **digital addiction** can be classified as actual diseases is still being discussed by psychologists. But something isn't quite right.

If your dad sucked an *actual* dummy every time he got bored, you'd be concerned (and probably creeped out). And if your grandma checked the letterbox 85 times a day, you'd call a doctor. If your aunty panicked if she left her alarm clock at home, you'd worry about her. But here we are – strapped to these devices **almost every minute** of our waking lives, constantly touching them or swiping them or staring at them. **We're hooked!**

addicted to being human

I want to pause here for a **reality check** – one of a few more to come in this book. Phones and the internet aren't bad. And really, a phone that isn't charged is just a hunk of metal and glass, and the internet is just a bunch of data stored on hard drives around the world. It's the way phones and the internet enable us to **connect with one another** that make them objectively some of the most *astonishingly* great things ever invented.

The human brain evolved over hundreds of thousands of years in the African savanna to run around grasslands, pick lice from our friends' hair, hunt wildebeest and go on adventures in small communities. Without the social skills to nurture friendships and build strong relationships, we'd likely starve, be eaten by a lion or find some other grisly, lonely end. That's why we are wired **so strongly** to cherish friendships, to check in on how others are responding to us and to stay up to date with what's going on.

But the world today is **very different** from the one humans evolved in. The internet is always on and we're no longer ever *out* of the conversation. We can always be publicly commented on, spoken to, laughed at or laughed with – 24/7. Something is always happening, which can *always* be checked by opening our phones.

Paired with apps trying to keep us as engaged as possible, the **hard-wired social habits** that strengthened our communities when we lived on ancient grasslands can keep us glued to our devices in the modern world

In time you'll become the expert on what online engagement you find rewarding, and what kind of online routines **work for you**. You can experiment with what feels right and listen to people around you for feedback (more on that soon).

Conversations on social media today are a little similar to sharing food and picking lice out of each other's hair, only digital, but it is worth knowing **how our brains change** after being online – and choose to act accordingly.

'I can chat to my friends anytime, and it's great.'
ULRIKA, 11

BRAINS ONLINE

When we're online and using digital tech a lot, our brains actually change. Johann Hari in his book *Stolen Focus* found that some of the biggest impacts are on our **ability to focus** and **get good sleep** – and both are really important.

focus

Phones and the internet let us do so many things at the *same time*, even on the *same screen*. You can be watching TV, messaging, playing games and shopping – **all at once**. Amazing!

But scientists have found that what we call **multitasking** is actually the brain switching between tasks every couple of seconds. It might *feel* like it saves us some time, but studies have found that multitasking can actually make us less efficient at what we're doing – and, over time, make us less creative or thoughtful because we've trained our brains to **think less deeply with less focus**.

sleep

Feeling tired sucks! **Sleep** is incredibly important for our health, but on average we sleep an hour *less* than people did a hundred years ago. More than a third of Australians get less than seven hours a night, which is the absolute **minimum recommended**. Technology has a role in this.

Watching TV, playing games, scrolling on socials and messaging can all keep your brain **alert and awake**. The **blue light** from screens makes it harder to go to sleep too by supressing **melatonin**, which is a hormone that your body releases at nighttime to help you feel sleepy.

So, if you're going to look at any screens after it's dark outside, try putting the device on **night mode** (which displays less blue light and more orange/red light) and **avoid watching** anything too exciting, scary or thrilling in the hour before going to bed.

chapter 4

SOCIAL (AND UNSOCIAL) MEDIA

Humans are the most social beings in the history of the planet! We *need* social connection and thrive when we have positive relationships. We've been communicating with each other since **forever** in so many ways: gesture, voice, music, dance, writing – and, since 1965, through computers.

Social media is any platform that allows people to communicate online as both **producers** (making content) and **consumers** (receiving content). This includes the obvious platforms like Instagram and YouTube, but also massively multiplayer online games like Fortnite and Minecraft, chatgroups like WhatsApp and Signal, and newsgroups and online communities like on Facebook.

Social media is now where we often get our news, stay up to date with friends, find entertainment, and learn about the world – and people **spend hours** on it every day.

THE BEST OF SOCIAL MEDIA

At its *best*, social media helps us connect with each other, build relationships, meet new people and learn about the world. Here are some of the **best bits**.

knowing what's going on

When your parents were young, the only way to get the news was to hear it on the radio, see it on the TV at night or read it in the newspaper in the morning. The only way to learn about what their friends were up to was to visit, write letters, call or hear stories through the grapevine.

Now, anyone can get **instant updates** on almost anything that is happening anywhere. A festival happening in the city? A party happening down the road? An unfolding global news event? People can now get up to speed with all of these sorts of things through the power of **social media** and **online news**.

staying in touch

Social media helps people **stay connected** even if they don't live in the same place or see each other regularly anymore. Phone numbers and addresses can change often, but the same social media accounts can be kept forever – and that means people can always find a way to get in touch.

connecting with people IRL

One of the best things about connecting online is its ability to help us **connect offline**. Community groups, interest groups, fan clubs, meet-up noticeboards, social sport apps and more all support people to connect and be active away from screens and the internet – together.

Research shows that spending time offline establishes and strengthens friendships **significantly more** than spending time together online.

'The best thing about social media is being able to see what your friends are doing and chat with people you know.'
HENRY, 13

togetherness in tricky times

In early 2020, COVID-19 began spreading around the world. In many countries (including Australia), public health efforts to stop the spread of the virus led to **restrictions** on how people could interact in person. Suddenly, depending on where they were in the world, some people weren't able to hang out with friends or family, go to movies or restaurants, play sports or go to school.

Even though some of us couldn't see each other IRL, the internet allowed us to **stay connected**. Social media especially let people talk to each other, engage with their local communities and generally stay in touch with the important people in their lives.

The internet also let many people in lockdown at home access **remote-learning** and **keep working** without having to *physically* go to school or work.

It's hard to overstate the importance of the internet and social media during this time. The **mental health impacts** of being isolated during the pandemic were real, but it's likely they would have been much worse without the internet and social media.

reaching the world

Social media can also support you to get a message out there. If you want to make a video, sing a song, teach something or say something, you can do it, write it, record it or film it and **put it online** for others to see. And, if it's something people are interested in and want to share, it can reach **the whole world!**

It can be possible (though definitely **not easy**) to make a career through social media too. If you make regular videos that get hundreds of thousands of views, for example, it's possible to **earn a living wage**. For those rare accounts with millions of followers, it's possible to make even more.

NOTE ON FAME

In 2024, a YouGov poll found 'gamer' tied with 'footballer' as the **most popular** career aspiration for children in the UK. And a third of kids surveyed across the US, the UK and China in 2019 reported that they wanted to be a YouTuber when they grew up.

Time for another **reality check**. To make the salary of a nurse or a firefighter as a YouTuber in Australia, you'd have to first qualify for **monetisation** on YouTube by getting 3 million Shorts views in the past 90 days and then make (on average) one video every week that gets 311,000 views (or one video each year that gets 16,000,000 views).

One of the tricky things about making money from social media is that it relies on being – and staying – **famous**. For every YouTuber that makes a living out of content creation, there are tens of thousands who put in the same effort and don't.

And, even if someone becomes famous, it doesn't mean they'll be **happy** or satisfied with their life. According to the long-running Harvard Study of Adult Development, it's **close relationships** that give people happiness – more than money or fame.

THE WORST OF SOCIAL MEDIA

Despite all the perks, studies show that social media use is having **negative effects** on people's mental health and wellbeing. This can be from cyberbullying, but also through well-intentioned interactions.

loneliness

Though it exists to help people to be more social, and more and more people are jumping on social media, Australians are reportedly **feeling more lonely**. A National Youth Mental Health Survey conducted by headspace found that **more than half of young people** feel a sense of loneliness, described as 'a lack of companionship some of the time/often'. This has been increasing over the past two decades.

'Social media can make you feel a little bit left out if you see your friends are doing something without you.'
JAY, 11

Seeing people doing things without us can make us feel left out or lonely – and that's **hard to avoid** on social media.

unhappiness

Staying connected and sharing experiences online can definitely make us happier, but the **World Happiness Report** found that 'adolescents who spend more time on electronic devices are less happy, and adolescents who spend more time on most other activities are happier'.

Additionally, researchers from the University of Michigan said that, although social media platforms like Facebook might seem to be a good way of 'fulfilling the basic human need for social connection', results from their own studies suggest that Facebook use may actually **undermine users' wellbeing**.

One of the biggest things those researchers found is that it's not just that time on social media can make us less happy; it's also that it can take over from the time spent on **non-screen activities** that generally do make us happier.

anxiety

We're feeling **more anxious** too!

According to the latest data from the Australian Bureau of Statistics, more than a third of young people are currently experiencing mental ill-health, and young women are more likely than young men to feel this way. It's also common for young people to **prefer staying at home** on a phone to going outside.

One in three Australian young people have experienced high or very high levels of distress in the past year, and studies consistently show a correlation between the amount of phone use and level of anxiety.

It isn't always clear what's driving higher levels of anxiety, but factors include **fear of negative evaluation** (people thinking or saying unkind things about you), **reduced sense of agency** (feeling your actions and their consequences are out of your control), **passive interaction** (like scrolling) without active engagement and exposure to **confusing misinformation**.

body image

In the past, we could really only **compare ourselves** with the people in our local area. On social media, we can instantly compare ourselves to **almost anyone** in the world – past, present, professionally photographed or AI-generated. It's impossible for us to *not* compare ourselves to the images we see, and this affects how we feel.

Social media companies are aware of this. Former Facebook data engineer Frances Haugen says that 32% of teen girls reported that Instagram made them **feel worse** when they felt bad about their bodies, and over 40% of Instagram users who felt 'unattractive' said that they started feeling that way when **using the app**.

Though social media companies have known this for some time, they kept their research **hidden from the public**. It was only through ex-employees like Frances that we were able to learn about it.

Today, a third of young people rate 'body image' as one of their top four personal concerns, and almost *everyone* retouches their photos in some way before posting.

Body dysmorphia is a mental illness where a person believes there is a flaw or defect in their body, leading to distress and repetitive behaviours. It now affects around 2% of the population, which is more than ever before.

'I've definitely seen people be mean about other people's appearances online.'
HARRISON, 11

We're unkind to other people about their bodies too: 90% of teenage girls and 65% of teenage boys have been **body-shamed** in the past year, often on social media.

WHAT'S GOING ON?

Social media companies don't say they want to make us feel lonely, anxious or ugly. Often, it's the **exact opposite**!

Here are their mission statements:

TikTok – 'to inspire creativity and bring joy'

YouTube – 'to give everyone a voice and show them the world'

Snapchat – 'an app that empowers people to express themselves, live in the moment, learn about the world, and have fun together'.

Sounds good, right? But behind these mission statements is a bigger goal: **to make as much money as possible** for the people who own these companies. They do this by keeping you engaged for as long as possible ... so that you can see more ads ... so they get paid more money by advertisers.

Almost all social media companies are paying the world's best software engineers megabucks to make their apps as engaging as possible. But the kicker is that the companies get paid whether you're laughing at your best friend's funny video or you're anxiously checking public comments on the photo you just uploaded – good or bad, the engagement **is the same to them**.

Being emotionally connected to your feed, anxious about your posts and worried about missing out all **drive engagement** – even more than positive connections that make you feel good.

This is because of **negativity bias**: a curious quirk of the brain that means we often give more weight to **negative feedback** than to **positive feedback**. This bias plays a role in how humans learn to be social, but it can be hijacked by social media companies aiming to increase engagement at all costs – and those costs are real and documented.

social media bans

Following concerns about the **negative impacts of social media** on the mental health and wellbeing of young people, governments around the world are exploring ways to keep young people **safe online**.

In 2024, the Australian Government decided to stop people **under the age of 16** signing up for social media accounts. To do so is now **against the law**. Age-verification is now being used to enforce this.

The list of banned platforms will change over time, but the short version is that young people under 16 aren't allowed on **most major platforms** like TikTok, Instagram, Facebook, Snapchat and X. Some messaging apps, online games and select video content will continue to be accessible in some way.

While this might be a relief for parents and carers, it can feel different for young people. As you already know, social media can provide connection, laughs and ideas. But there is also the possibility for **real harm**, like bullying, addiction or being exposed to inappropriate content.

Methods of **age verification** will evolve, and they might not always be unbreakable. The responsibility for ensuring young people don't get on social media rests with the platforms – for now. And young people or their guardians won't be punished if they're found using them. That said, these laws are designed to keep you safe, and breaking the law can have serious consequences. So, it's strongly encouraged that you **don't lie about your age**.

MAKING SOCIAL MEDIA WORK FOR YOU

If you do find yourself on social media, here are some tips to make it work for you:

- **Only use the apps that make you feel good** and help you connect with people IRL. Avoid apps that make you feel anxious or worse about yourself.
- **Unfollow or mute accounts** that make you feel annoyed, bad or upset.
- **Build a positive feed.** Find accounts that make you feel good and inspire you (including in non-appearance-based or fame-based ways).
- **Follow people you admire** for their interests and passions.
- **Balance your time online** with IRL interactions and activities.

chapter 5

GAME ON OR GAME OVER?

Humans *love* **playing games**. From tiggy and footy to cards and chess, we've always loved playing in friendly (and sometimes not-so-friendly!) competition with others. We play games to pass time, connect with teammates and opponents, improve our skills, and have a laugh. It's also a key way that we **learn**.

In the past, we used to only be able to play with people in **meat space** – the 3D world around us. We could only play soccer with someone on the same field or cards with someone sitting at the same table. But computers and the internet now let us play games in ways that were completely unimaginable a generation ago.

'It's like being alive in another world with your friends.'
JINGWEI, 11

We can now play games like Scrabble online – but we can also go on a **massively multi-player quest** to slay a treasure-hoarding dragon on a far-off planet. Games can let us connect in real time with people **all around the world** – and friends just up the street.

And beyond just being fun or letting you connect with other people, games can also help to build your teamwork and problem-solving skills, sharpen your hand–eye coordination and much more. Just like a good book can take you on an **imaginative journey** into another world, so can a good game. Within a game, however, you can even *write* your own story – and other peoples' too.

HOW TO WIN WHILE GAMING

There are so many **incredible experiences** and connections to find through gaming. But, just like on social media and the rest of the internet, there are things going on *behind* the screens that it's important to be aware of.

game time

Playing games online is one of the biggest ways Australians spend their **free time**. Over three-quarters of adolescents in Australia play electronic games **every day**, and nearly one in three kids in Australia plays computer-based games for more than 2 hours a day. Some games have become so good at capturing our attention that we can't find time to do much else!

And while Fortnite, Minecraft, Roblox and Candy Crush are very different to one other, what is similar is how incredibly engaging they aim to be.

In 2022, the World Health Organization recognised **internet gaming disorder** – a condition where gaming time takes over the other things you need to do to be healthy (like getting enough sleep, being active and connecting IRL) – for the first time. Adults are at risk too. The Royal Australian College of General Practitioners estimates 6–11% of Western adults have some level of internet gaming disorder.

'My brother, when my parents ask him to finish playing Roblox, he gets really grumpy.'
JESSIE, 11

who's being played?

Much like social media, even though many online games are free to play, they make **billions of dollars** every year. While some games sell ads, the money generally comes from extras and add-ons – like buying battle plans, V-Bucks, Minecoins and character packs.

It can be helpful to remember that the aim of most gaming platforms is to make as much money as possible by keeping you engaged and wanting to **play more**. They can do this by making exciting games and also by creating a space to hang out with your friends and others.

But **your wellbeing**, particularly away from the screen, isn't their priority.

'I don't want to miss out when my friends are going on a quest together – it feels like letting them down.'
LACHLAN, 13

game chats

Most online games let you **chat** with the people you're playing with via text, audio or video. And, just like with social media, there are great conversations to be had – be that with people you know or with people you meet. But it's also important to **stay safe** when online chatting through games.

One in five young people have experienced **in-game bullying** – and that can be just as hurtful and harmful as bullying on social media or in person.

eSports

'We talk about the game but also everything else.'
AMARA, 13

The world's best footballers and rockstars have sponsors and promo deals and millions of followers around the world, and so do the world's **best gamers**. eSports is now a billion-dollar **global industry** and things are only *just* taking off.

$

Whether you're playing Fortnite or Minecraft or any other online game, you're able watch many of the world's most famous players play in real time at the **highest level**. Platforms like Twitch, YouTube, Facebook Gameroom and heaps more allow you to stream games around the world, chat with commentators and players, get tips, learn cheats and ways to unlock extra features – and, just like with socials, you can do it all for *free*.

But, just like with socials, when you're getting something for free, very often **you are the product**. Most eSports platforms use your interests (built from your data and metadata) to show you ads that they get paid for.

Again, there's not necessarily anything wrong with this, but it's worth knowing that each platform's aim is to make you as engaged as possible so that they can get paid to show you more ads. Your **health, happiness and wellbeing** aren't really part of their equation.

PLAYING IRL

The games we love playing online are often based on things we love to do offline. If you want to replace some screen time with green time, check out some real-world alternatives:

- **Love building shelters in Minecraft? Maybe collect some wood, rope and tools, and make a bushcraft shelter in your backyard.**
- **Interested in shooting games like Fortnite? Maybe check out where your nearest archery range is and learn how to shoot targets using a bow and arrow.**
- **What about Mario Kart? See if there's a bike co-op nearby that can help you build a billycart.**

It's true that you can't find dragons or fly to space or bend the laws of physics. Alternatives aren't always quick or easy to find, and some do have costs, but you can often find something brilliant IRL that scratches the same itch as your favourite game.

MAKING GAMING WORK FOR YOU

We talk more about how to be healthy with tech in Chapter 7, but here are some specific tips to help make gaming work for you:

- Set up agreed **switch-off times** with your family in advance (e.g., through your Family Technology Agreement).
- If you're playing games with mates, **share the timelines** you're working with. It can be helpful to decide these together too (e.g., 'If we play games, it's for an hour between 5 pm and 6 pm on Wednesdays and Fridays').
- If you're playing with people you don't know, use a **screen name** that isn't your real name.
- Turn off the **chat function** if you don't like the conversation.
- Report **inappropriate behaviour** and **cyberbullying** to moderators.
- **Don't share passwords** to your accounts.
- **Enable safety controls** on devices and games.
- Get permission from your parents or carers for **all in-game purchases**.

'It feels like you're building something together with the people you play with.'
CORA, 10

- If you see another gamer being treated badly, **don't pile on**. And, if you feel able to, stand up for them.
- If you feel like you or someone you know might be gaming too much, talk to a trusted adult and check out **gamequitters.com** for help.

chapter 6

(E)SAFETY FIRST

There is a *lot* of content on the internet – and it's growing by more than 300 million terabytes every day! Most of what you come across will be informative, entertaining, fun, social, helpful and more. But some of what's on the internet is **harmful, offensive or illegal**. Some of it is intended only for adults. And some of it can make you feel *yuck*.

A PLACE TO START

In a world-first, Australia appointed an **eSafety Commissioner** – Julie Inman Grant – to help us have safer and more **positive experiences online**. I spoke with Julie for this book, and she had this to say:

> *There's a lot of great things you can do on the internet, but sometimes we see people behaving badly online. We want people to have fun, to learn and be engaged, but above all be safe.*
>
> **—Julie Inman Grant, eSafety Commissioner**

Most government websites are *terrible*, but the eSafety website is actually **brilliant**. It's informative, clear and helpful – and it has information about pretty much every app, game and possible hazard on the internet. It also has tips on privacy, reporting inappropriate content and generally staying safe. It's so good that I *really* think you should **check it out** for yourself: **eSafety.gov.au**.

THE LAW

Just like the laws that help us stay safe in the physical world, there are laws that help us stay safe online too. Beyond age restrictions, what people do, say and post online on any platform can be illegal, and police take this seriously.

Just like the G, PG, M and MA 15+ ratings on movies, the government also has online content **classfications**:

content that should be **freely accessible** to people of any age (like the news or Wikipedia)

content that is considered **inappropriate** (and restricted) for people under 18 (like nude or explicit images, videos, or pornography)

content that is **illegal** to host or access anywhere in Australia (like violent content, abuse or terrorist acts).

If there is any content about you online that is considered cyberbullying, or if a private or nude image or video of you is shared without your consent, you (or an adult) can contact the police or the eSafety Commission directly and they can help you get it taken down.

YOUR SAFETY NETWORK

To help you stay safe, put together a safety network of 3–5 adults that you can talk to openly about *anything* that happens online. At least one of these adults should be from outside your family, and at least one should live outside your home – like a teacher, coach or good friend's parent.

The adults in your safety network need to know how important it is to listen to and believe you if something bad happens. They should also know some of the next steps they can help you with if things go wrong or you need help in any way – you can share this chapter and the eSafety website with them too.

It's worth having early conversations with your safety network about the role you'd like them to play in helping you stay safe and avoid some of the harms that we cover in the next couple of pages.

illegal and restricted content

It's pretty easy to accidentally come across **inappropriate content** online. Someone might send you an image or link to something that doesn't feel right. You might come across disturbing content on your own.

> 'Even just having one letter wrong in a word in a search can lead you to see something that you're not wanting to see.'
> **OLIVE, 12**

When your body experiences something stressful, frightening or dangerous, there are several **natural responses** that can kick in. Seeing disturbing content online might trigger any one or more of these responses:

Fight – becoming angry or upset and taking action (like telling an adult).

Flight – getting out of the situation by shutting down the app or browser, and maybe trying to forget what you saw.

Freeze – being unable to respond or do anything, like you can't stop looking even though you want to.

Fawn – pretending that what you're seeing is normal and not upsetting, and trying to justify why or how you're seeing it.

Any or all of these reactions are **valid and normal**. There's no 'wrong' way to respond, and they have all served different evolutionary purposes – and still do for many animals in the wild! People can even cycle through a few of them over a period of time.

No matter what, you shouldn't have to be exposed to **disturbing content** – particularly when you're a kid!

You can get help if you feel upset or uneasy after seeing something online that you didn't want to see. Here are some things you can do.

Talk to someone you trust.

The first step is to **talk to someone in your safety network** about what you've seen and how it has made you feel. After this, you can talk about how you came across the content and steps you can take in the future to **protect yourself** and others.

Get help and support.

Beyond your safety network, you can also call (or chat online with) **Kids Helpline** on 1800 55 1800, and older kids can contact **headspace** on 1800 650 890. These services provide **free confidential counselling** for *any* issue – including things that happen online.

Check your privacy and access settings.

You can set privacy, content and SafeSearch settings on most apps, browsers, search engines and devices to help keep you from seeing disturbing content. Most social media platforms have some form of **sensitive content control** for your feed. (Check eSafety.gov.au for more information for any particular app.)

Report and block inappropriate content on the platform.

You can **confidentially report** inappropriate content and behaviour to almost all apps, as they have responsibilities to their users – particularly users under 18. Reporting can help keep the platform safe for others too.

Report it to eSafety.gov.au or the police.

If someone sends you disturbing content via a link, or you find inappropriate content where it shouldn't be, you can report it to eSafety.gov.au. If you come across illegal content online, you should report this to the police through **Crimestoppers** on **1800 333 000**. Remember, in an emergency dial 000.

communicating with people you don't know

Some websites, apps and games let you text or video-chat with people you don't know. This can be fun! Finding out **common interests** with someone who lives on the other side of the world/city/country *is* amazing, but it's wise to be careful. While most people are just looking for connection, not everyone online is being honest about who they are or what they want – and that can be **dangerous**.

Here are some tips to stay safe:

- **Be careful with what you share** and stay truthful about your age. It's better to not give away any specific details about your life (for example, which school you go to) and keep a conversation light until you know the person more. Lying about your age can get you into situations that are seriously not okay.
- **Don't chat with adults** unless you have a trusted adult present. Be careful when chatting with other young people too. (Are you sure they are young?) Without people you both know being around, situations can quickly become inappropriate or potentially illegal.
- **Be confident in your rights** – to consent, to say no and to not be abused. Consent is important. It's always okay to say no – even to a conversation. It's never okay to be made to do or say something you're uncomfortable with. It's never okay to receive or share personal photos without consent. Remember, your consent can be withdrawn at any time too.
- **Be particularly careful** if the conversation moves to personal topics or to another platform. Check in on how you are feeling, what you are consenting to and how confident you are that the person is who they say they are.

'You can get weird messages from people that you don't know.'
BRIANNA, 11

- **Trust your instincts**, and know how and when to exit. If something doesn't feel right, it probably isn't. Remember it's always okay to cut off contact straightaway. This can sometimes be as easy as just closing the browser and not going back for a while. You can also tell the person to not contact you again, or you can block them so they can't get in contact – most apps have this feature. If neither of these things work, then it's likely a form of cyber-bullying, which you don't have to put up with.

The general advice is that, until you're an adult, you **shouldn't** meet people IRL who you've only met online without a trusted adult with you. (Having someone you trust with you when you meet someone for the first time is a good idea at any age!) As well as having a **trusted adult** with you, the eSafety Commissioner's tips for young people include:

- **Share your plans** with other people. (You can even share your live location with apps such as Find My Friends on Apple or Google Maps on Android.)
- Arrange any meeting in a **busy public place**, and don't go somewhere else.
- Have a **predetermined 'out'**, with a time limit and place to be after the catch up, and communicate this at the start.

If you feel uncomfortable or unsafe or something feels suspicious, don't worry about hurting the person's feelings or coming across as 'rude' – **just get out of there**. You can message or call your safety network and **find somewhere safe** (like a busy place) to wait until they can come get you.

cyberbullying

Cyberbullying is when someone uses the internet to be mean to another person. It can include hurtful, abusive or humiliating posts, images, comments, messages, chats, videos – anything online. It can also be someone impersonating you **without your consent** or making new accounts to repeatedly contact you after they've been blocked. Things that would be considered **bullying IRL** are considered **cyberbullying** if they happen online.

IMAGE-BASED ABUSE

Someone sharing a nude or intimate image or video of someone without their consent is called image-based abuse – and it's illegal.

It's still image-based abuse if it's a screenshot of a live chat (sometimes called capping), a meme or an AI-generated deepfake of you, or if it's a part-nude. Images and videos can also be classified as intimate if they show someone without the religious or cultural clothes that they would normally wear in public.

You should never share nudes. However, if one gets out somehow by accident, you can still seek help: from your safety network, from the eSafety Commissioner or from the police.

what to do

If cyberbullying happens to you, here are some steps that you can take:

> 'I was on a group chat where someone pretended to be me, and said things that I would never say.'
> JUNE, 11

- **Remember it's not your fault.** The person doing the cyberbullying is in the wrong.
- **Ask them to stop.** If you feel safe to do so, ask the person to stop or change their behaviour. This clearly establishes that you're not okay with what's going on.
- **If they don't stop, resist the urge to respond.** Bullying behaviour often feeds off someone's reactions. Try your best to not respond to any hateful things targeted at you online.
- **Tell a trusted adult.** Even if it can be hard, talking about it with someone you trust helps you to be safe, not feel alone, regain control of the situation and take the next steps.
- **Collect evidence of inappropriate behaviour.** This should include who shared it, when and on what site or platform it was shared. What was the URL? Screenshots or recordings can help with the eSafety Commission or the police.

- **Report the behaviour.** For image-based abuse, you can report it straightaway to eSafety and the police. The team there can help have the intimate images or videos removed quickly, *even* if it's going viral. You can also report if someone's behaviour is making you feel unsafe, or if they are asking you to do inappropriate things.
- **Prevent further contact.** Block or mute them. Most apps and platforms allow you to do this immediately. If you have reported behaviour to the police or eSafety, they should advise you when is the most appropriate time to block them – this can help you collect more evidence if you need to.

being an upstander not a bystander

One of the most powerful things you can do to combat inappropriate online behaviour is to **call it out** when you see it. This takes courage, but if you feel confident and safe, any positive action you take can really make a difference. It can help the person being bullied and show others what to do if they also know someone who is being bullied.

Things you can do to help someone who is experiencing cyberbullying or image-based abuse:

- **Direct message the person**, if you know them, to show your support.
- **Help them to avoid engaging** with trolls or reacting where unhelpful.

- **Help them to report it**, and let them know about their options.
- **Speak up** or show you disagree with disrespectful behaviour online. A thumbs-down emoji on a hurtful comment, or saying, 'This is not cool,' can let people know what you think and help stop inappropriate behaviour.

Professor Amanda Third from Western Sydney University provides advice to the United Nations on **digital rights** for young people, and she has this to say:

> *When you know something isn't right, don't stay quiet – tell someone! Be brave – you might have to upskill your parents or your teachers – there are people around you that don't get it, but you have a lot to share and teach.*

chapter 7

BEING HEALTHY WITH TECH

The 2023 **World Happiness Report** found that young people who spend more time on the internet, listening to music online, on social media and playing computer games are **generally less happy** than those that spend more time getting adequate sleep, playing sports, exercising and having in-person social interactions.

There's no one-size-fits-all approach to **tech use and happiness**, and you're the best judge of what makes you feel good, but here are some tips on making your time online as **positive** as possible.

'I like playing games on my iPad, and also games on phones.'
RORY, 11

SET UP A FAMILY TECH AGREEMENT

One way to navigate conversations about using technology at home is through a **family tech agreement**. This is where everyone in your household (including adults) commits to healthy tech use by first talking about what healthy use looks like and then deciding **how to respond** if things get unhealthy.

The agreement can cover time limits, the types of tech that can be used, privacy commitments and much more. The nice thing is that it's not a one-way agreement; it's for **everyone** in the household, so kids can call out their parents on healthy tech use too!

It's important that the whole family gets together to make this agreement so it's specific to everyone's needs and ideas about healthy tech use.

There are plenty of **great templates** available online (for example, on the eSafety website and on **behindthescreens.me**). There's also a sample agreement, in which kids and adults commit to use tech in appropriate and healthy ways, on the next couple of pages.

Commitment	Kids	Adults
I will aim to spend no more than ____ on tech per day that isn't work or homework related.	1.5 hours	2.5 hours
If I see or experience something that isn't okay online I will:	Tell a trusted adult.	Report it if required through the appropriate channels.
I will only use devices in:	Shared spaces.	Appropriate spaces.
When my tech time is up, I will:	Wrap up my activity and put away my device within 5 minutes.	Wrap up my activity and put my device on silent or do-not-disturb.
If someone says I am spending too much time with tech I will:	Listen carefully.	Listen carefully.
My completely tech-free times are:	8:30 pm–7 am every night; 6 pm–7 am Tuesday nights and October weeknights.	10 pm–6 am every night; 7 pm–6 am Tuesday nights and October weeknights.
During tech-free times I won't use:	Tablets, computers, games, phones.	Tablets, computers, phones placed on do-not-disturb.
I will not give out my or my family's private information without permission.	Yes	Yes

I will take care of the device(s) I'm using and tell my family if it's broken, stolen, or lost. If I lose or break a device I understand those consequences.	Yes	Yes
I will share my tech times and tech-free times with:	The people I game with, other friends.	My work colleagues, other families in our community.
I know that not everything I read, hear or see online is true. I will consider whether a source or author is credible.	Yes	Yes
If location-tracking is enabled on a device:	I will be told how and when it will be used.	I will share how and when it will be used.
I will:	Talk openly and honestly about my tech use and anything I might be struggling with online.	Listen to kids first, recognise that media is a big part of young peoples' lives even if I don't understand why, and embrace this world.
Signature Date		

TIPS FOR HEALTHY USE

The good news is that there are some simple things you can do if you feel like you're on devices more than you'd like, or if you'd like to have more healthy interactions with technology.

1. **Stop the dings!** So that you're not continually brought back to your devices when you're doing something else, try these strategies:
   - Turn off **notifications** (and alerts, dings, badges etc.) from your apps and devices.
   - Enable **focus mode** during the day to allow call and message notifications from only a few people, such as parents or carers.
   - Switch on **sleep** or **do-not-disturb mode** to help you avoid tech use at least 2 hours before you plan to go to sleep.
   - Keep your devices **out of sight** and off your body.

2. **Spend time offline.** It's important to balance screen time with time offline. It might be tricky to start with, but here are some suggestions:

- Be aware of when you are and aren't using tech. Turn on Apple's **Screen Time** or Android's **Digital Wellbeing** feature on your phone, and set time limits for other devices to keep track of and control how much you're online. You might even try a physical, timed lockbox (like a KSafe) if you want to get really serious.
- Regularly carve out some **time away from tech**. You can do this by leaving your devices at home when you go somewhere (make sure your parents or carers know and are okay with this, of course) or spending time out of reception, deep in the outdoors.
- Try out the **analogue versions** of things you use tech for every day. That could mean trying out an actual alarm clock, following a physical street map, playing a board game with friends, using a wall calendar, listening to the radio, reading a book … the list goes on!
- Check out **offtober.org** for some more ideas on how to go offline regularly with community.

'Sometimes during the holidays my parents let me have unlimited screen time – and I had like 10 hours in one day, but it did feel like too much.'
JON, 11

3. **Eat your digital greens.** Just as you think about physical nutrition (what foods you eat and how much), you should also think about, in the words of psychologist Jocelyn Brewer, your 'digital nutrition'.

- Make sure you get enough **digital greens** (like engaging with meaningful and nourishing content and learning new skills) alongside your **digital sugar hits** (like scrolling and gaming).
- Be **mindful, meaningful and moderate** with what you do online. Just like eating too much junk food can make you feel ill, spending too much time on one app or activity can make you feel not great too. It's not that you shouldn't eat junk food ever, just that it's all about balance. Ways to do this include:
    - only being on apps that make you **feel good** about yourself and help you connect with people IRL
    - avoiding apps that make you **feel anxious and worse** about yourself
    - finding content that makes you **feel good and inspired** (including in non-appearance-based and non-fame-based ways). Follow people that you admire for their interests and passions.

FINDING FLOW

You know when you're doing something you enjoy and time just flies – you become fully absorbed in what you're doing and you feel great? Psychologists call this a **flow state**, and often it's when we're in a flow state that we feel most present, fulfilled and alive.

If you can find flow through an activity or hobby IRL and offline, it's a **big win** for your health and you're *way* less likely to be reaching for your device every few minutes.

Some people find flow by being creative with art or music, building things, playing sports, rock-climbing, solving puzzles, surfing, crafting, gardening – there are *heaps* of ways!

Where do **you** find your flow?

know the signs of unhealthy tech use

It's important to know the signs of **unhealthy** tech use. Tune in to how you feel and check in with your mind. When you're on tech or have just got off it, is your mind racing and anxious, or is it calm and relaxed? Your body can give you signals too. Are you tense when you're using certain kinds of tech? Are your shoulders hunched and muscles tight? How does that feel: **good or bad?**

If you or someone close to you are concerned about how much time you're spending with tech – whether its gaming, chatting, scrolling, whatever – a helpful thing to think about is **what you're giving up IRL** to spend time with tech and how that's affecting you.

Try asking yourself these questions:

- Are you on your devices **late at night**?
- Are you finding it hard to get to sleep at night because your mind is still **buzzing**?
- Do you get **annoyed** when someone interrupts you when you're online or asks you to stop?
- Are you **putting off** getting schoolwork done but still spending lots of time on tech?
- Do you feel **tense, sad or deflated** as a result of what you're doing online?
- Do you try to **get out of commitments** so you can spend more time on your device?
- Are you **missing out** on exercise, playing sport or IRL social connections because you're spending so much time online?
- Is it **hard to know** when enough tech is enough?

If you answered **yes** to any of these questions, you may be spending too much time online or with tech – and you might need some support.

THE BIGGER PICTURE ABOUT BEING HEALTHY

While there are plenty of things you can do to be healthier with tech, many aren't easy in practice. They may also require effort, money and time. And, even if you give them a good go, it's common to slip back into **old habits**.

Remember: **this isn't your fault.** It's how apps and the internet are *designed* to work. Many of the world's richest companies have made fortunes by getting us to engage online with their platforms – again and again and again.

Switching off tech isn't just about **unplugging**. It's about what you're **replacing** tech time with. If you *really* want to get off tech, the best, most effective and enduring solutions involve making your offline world **more nourishing** than the online world, to make IRL connections stronger and more enriching than online ones, and to understand and reshape what might be compelling you to go online in the first place.

chapter 8

WHAT TO BELIEVE

Most people have a **spidey sense** for what to believe in the real world and it generally works on the internet too. Bogus news article? Someone pulling a prank? Glamorous selfie? We're pretty good at knowing when we *aren't* seeing the full (or real) picture.

It's even easier to spot **legit information** when we're being taught something. Want to fix a flat bike tyre, play 'Blackbird' on guitar or build a worm farm? There are thousands of helpful videos online showing you how. No-one is trying to **fool you** – and the proof is in the pudding.

But what happens if you want to find out who Jar Jar Binks from Star Wars *really* was, if people *did* actually land on the moon or what the impacts of climate change are?

There are *lots* of different opinions about these and other topics – some reasonable, some bogus. How do we know **what** to believe? And **who** should we believe?

ALGORITHMS ARE CHOOSING MORE OF WHAT WE SEE

One reason why it's getting harder to know what to believe is because our news and social feeds are increasingly controlled by **algorithms** – a set of instructions that websites and apps use to increase your use of their platform. These instructions are written by computer programmers with the main aim to keep us engaged on a website for as long as possible (to make more money through advertising).

These algorithms are often *really* good – and they're getting better all the time too, because they're being **trained by you**! Algorithms learn from your data and metadata how to keep you (and everyone else) engaged longer and longer.

It's as if you liked the buttery-sweetness of your chocolate birthday cake, and the recipe learnt that, and then **adjusted itself** to include more butter and sugar every time you baked it, on and on and on, until the ingredients were just butter and sugar – and that makes caramel, not chocolate cake!

That's a funny example, but when algorithms train themselves on **user behaviour** it can have **strange consequences** for what videos you watch on the internet, the music you listen to, the words you write (through predictive text, for example) and even what news you see about the world.

what is an algorithm?

An algorithm is just **a set of instructions** that can be followed. Like the steps for tying your shoelaces, baking a chocolate cake or dividing 36,296 by 13.

Computers *love* algorithms. Every computer program you can think of is just a **giant algorithm machine**. Inputs go in, algorithms do their thing, outputs come out. A calculator has a good algorithm for dividing numbers by other numbers, the *Australian Women's Weekly Children's Birthday Cake Book* has good chocolate cake algorithms, and social media companies have great algorithms for showing you what you want to see, *generally* with the goal of keeping you engaged.

For example, the algorithm Instagram uses to choose what post to show you next might code for things like:

review the time you (and people like you) have looked at all posts on the platform, and how many likes or shares the posts have | find the posts from people you care about that will make you engage more actively | check what else is relevant about you at this particular time (websites you visited recently, time of day/night, recent activities) | crosscheck with the likelihood of you engaging with other posts (epic-fail video? music artist? viral pranks? cat videos?) | rank all possible posts in order of engagement-score | show the highest-ranking posts (but save some good ones to appear when it looks like you might switch to a different app) ...

The actual algorithms used by any social media company are made up of thousands of lines of computer code – and they're **closely guarded secrets**.

It's great! If you're interested in K-pop, your feed will show you music, news and stories about K-pop stars. Same with snowboarding, baking, Fortnite, bike riding, VR, art history ... whatever! There's an **endless scroll** of relevant information, just waiting to be consumed.

FAKE NEWS

In 2017, a story about 'US Bacon Reserves' hitting a 50-year low was covered by news outlets around the world, leading to stockpiling of bacon and an increase in bacon prices. The trouble was that it was just a **marketing ploy** from the Ohio Pork Council!

And in 2020, **fake news** about a link between 5G phone towers and COVID-19 spread around the world and led to protesters setting phone towers *on actual fire* in Europe.

What's worrying is that fake news tends to **spread faster and further** than real news. Researchers analysing 12 years of data on what was then called Twitter (now X) found posts containing falsehoods spread 6 times faster than truthful posts and reached more than 10 times as many people! This is because when humans see something shocking, we're like, **'Say whaaat???'** and we're more likely to share it around without realising (or even considering whether) it's fake.

'I try to look for where the website comes from. Like, if it ends with ".gov.au" then you know it comes from the government, but if it's ".com" then it's from somewhere that is trying to make money.'
HENRY, 13

MISINFORMATION

There's a difference between genuine mistakes, when people unwittingly get the facts wrong – this is called misinformation – and when people *deliberately* spread false information to mislead others – this is called disinformation. Both are incorrect and both considered 'fake', but knowing whether incorrect information is an accident or shared on purpose can help us understand more about an issue. More and more fake news is being generated all the time, by people and now increasingly by AI – sometimes with real consequences.

HOW TO TELL REAL NEWS FROM FAKE NEWS

On social media and the internet more broadly, news and information is shown with the principle of **equivalence**. That means that when posts are shared, they all look the same – whether they originally came from the ABC, *Teletubbies* or the *Betoota Advocate* (a satire website). This means that it's up to readers to determine what is **reputable and believable**, and what might be **fake**.

Beyond **trusting your gut** (which is usually pretty good), there are a lot of principles to help you decide whether or not to believe something you see online.

who benefits?

The ancient Romans had a question they asked to figure out what to believe: **'Cui bono?'** – meaning **'Who benefits?'**

People and organisations often put out information that ultimately benefits them. This is often by making them more money, but it can also be to increase **influence** or **reputation** (which may then be used to make money). For example:

- If a **newspaper company** makes money from advertisers that put ads in the paper, they'll make content that gets more people to buy the paper so that more advertisers pay to advertise with them.
- If an **influencer** makes money from companies that sponsor their content (known as 'sponcon'), the more followers they get the more sponsorship money they receive. This can 'influence' influencers to put out content that makes people engage more, whether or not it's accurate, helpful, balanced or truthful.
- If an **organisation** makes money from donations – e.g., saving koala habitats – they'll likely put out information that raises awareness of their cause (like how much logging is taking place) to get more donations in the future.

This doesn't mean that all information coming from someone who is benefitting is fake, just that it's important to **think about why** they're publishing that information – because *sometimes* people will bend or filter the truth to reach their goals.

More recently, platforms like X, Instagram and YouTube have been shown to be **tweaking their algorithms** to prioritise or deprioritise different news stories based on government orders. In many cases it's to support safety online and to remove harmful or illegal content, but it isn't always clear how platforms' algorithms are influenced by their owners either. Moderation of normal content is very likely happening behind the screens.

extraordinary claims require extraordinary evidence

If you said, 'I ate an apple this morning,' an apple core in the compost would generally be enough **evidence** for someone to believe you.

But if you said, 'I saw an *alien* this morning,' you'd need to provide some **extraordinary evidence** to convince someone. Would a blurry photo of some unidentifiable object flying in the sky be enough? Maybe a video of you shaking hands with something alien-looking?

The idea that extraordinary claims require extraordinary evidence was popularised by Carl Sagan, and it can help us decide what to believe of what we read in the news, see on the internet and hear more generally.

CONSPIRACY THEORIES

Earth is flat. Humans never landed on the moon. COVID-19 was caused by 5G mobile towers. How do we know what to believe? And when is something a conspiracy?

It's helpful to use the principle extraordinary claims require extraordinary evidence as your guide. What evidence do you need to believe or disbelieve these statements? And from whom?

Conspiracy theories often include the *additional* extraordinary claim that lots of people are actively hiding the truth. This additional extraordinary claim should also require additional extraordinary evidence.

consider the source

It's helpful to always check the **original source** of the information. Government sources (websites with **.gov.au** at the end), the publicly funded ABC (**abc.net.au**) and publicly funded schools and universities (**.edu.au**) are funded *by* the public to benefit the public – which *should* make them **trustworthy**. Government bodies, schools and universities have responsibilities to be truthful and informative, and have a bunch of checks and balances built in to make sure information is **accurate and evidence based**. They are a good place to start.

But while we can *generally* believe information from governments, academics or public institutions, it's okay to apply these principles to **public authoritative information** too.

CONFIRMATION BIAS, ECHO CHAMBERS AND POLARISATION

Humans typically like hanging out with people who agree with us and seeing things that **affirm our beliefs**. It's called **confirmation bias** and everyone acts on it without even thinking about it – even online.

When we see things in our news feeds that we really agree with, we tend to engage with it more. We also engage when we see things we strongly disagree with: stuff that makes us angry, scared, protective or emotional. Either way – and regardless of the truth – the algorithm 'wins'.

Before the internet, it was difficult to tailor messages just for *you*. Newspapers could be read by **anyone**, and **everyone** could tune in to the 7 pm news. This made it harder for anyone to put out information that was **outrageously fake**, because someone would call it out before long.

It's very different now with **algorithm-generated feeds**. Content can now be **targeted** to very specific audiences. For example, the Flat Earth Society can promote flat-earth videos on Facebook to people who believe in chemtrails. The Save the Whales Society can target whale videos exclusively to people who eat plant-based diets.

A risk of this is that we end up only seeing things that we **already believe and agree with** and communicating only with people who think similarly to us. This is called an **echo chamber**, and it means that it's really difficult to even come across different ideas or perspectives.

Over time, this **polarises** us – that's where people have very strongly held views on **extreme sides** of debates, and conversations often become shouting matches between people who think the other side are absolute losers. We are seeing polarisation around the world for lots of issues like gender and sexuality, racism, health and politics.

How can we tell if we're being polarised? It isn't easy. But if something seems like it's made for a **very specific audience**, doesn't consider **other perspectives** or **ridicules** the other side, it *might* not be fair, balanced or true at all. Where people **passionately disagree** with each other, it's helpful to ask: 'What do the *best* people on the other side think?' and 'What information are they seeing?'

Frances Haugen, a former data scientist at Facebook, says:

> *What you find is that when people are sent targeted misinformation to a community, it can make it hard to reintegrate into wider society because now you don't have shared facts.*

If we aren't exposed to **good ideas** from people we wouldn't normally agree with, or we can't even agree on **shared facts**, what does it mean for our ability to work together?

In the words of Professor Amanda Third:

> *You're going to have to fight hard to keep different ideas in front of you. Talk to your peers about what you're seeing and what they're seeing. You're going to have to decide what's right for you, and will have to work with others to decide together what's right for everyone.*

TRUST YOURSELF!

So, how do you know what you can trust? The best you can do is to apply these principles and, ultimately, **trust yourself**.

You can have some influence over some algorithms or try and 'train them' over time by choosing what you look at or what you click on. On certain platforms and apps, you can even **delete your data** and start again!

It's important to know, though, that this algorithm can be **altered or influenced by others**: for example, if advertisers pay for targeted ads, or if a platform wants to prioritise or deprioritise specific kinds of content, such as news. The information that keeps us most *engaged* isn't necessarily the information that's **truthful or fair**. Often it's the opposite.

It's worth remembering this, and to remind yourself to occasionally seek out content that isn't chosen for you by an algorithm. This means not just always following the suggestions of the platforms.

Your spidey sense is often pretty good. If something doesn't seem right, it probably isn't. If someone sounds like they're just trying to make money, it's likely that they are. If something sounds too good to be true, it probably is.

That's not to say don't believe *anything*. Most of what is out there *is* published with **good intent**, but a little **scepticism** and **critical thinking** is healthy.

The bottom line is this: the more aware you are of potential sources of misinformation and disinformation, the more critically you'll be able to **decide what to believe** for yourself.

chapter 9

ARTIFICIAL INTELLIGENCE AND YOU

Can computers **think**? Will they ever be **conscious**? How could we ever tell?

Ever since the first electronic computers were built in the 1900s, it was clear that they could do some things a lot faster than humans. Divide 1888053925669 by 97340? Write the word 'computer' a million times? Calculate the position of Jupiter on 8 March 2976? All doable by early computers in the blink of an eye.

Gradually, computers have been able to do more and more things faster than humans. And they're increasingly able to do more **'human'** things too.

Creating letters, essays, drawings, songs, videos – you name it: almost anything humans can create and share online, AI is now trying to make. **Humanoid robots** and other **AI-enabled machines** are trying to replicate what humans do in the physical world too.

In 1950, a British mathematician named **Alan Turing** proposed a test: if you can't tell the difference between a machine and a human in a normal conversation, then we should say that it can 'think'. He figured that if you had a normal conversation with a human you'd never stop to wonder if the human was 'thinking', and that it shouldn't be any different for a computer. This is called the **Turing test**, and online chatbots can now pass it easily!

Does this mean computers can **actually think**? Maaaybe ...

AI IN OUR WORLD

Computers can certainly do so many things now that it can feel like they have what's called **artificial intelligence** (AI). Scientists think about AI as having **three levels**:

1. **Artificial narrow intelligence** – doing a specific task really well. AI smashes this out of the park today with tasks like doing maths, playing chess, manufacturing things ... The list grows every day.

2. **Artificial general intelligence** – thinking, understanding and acting like a human would. AI is getting pretty close with tasks like driving a car, writing essays and answering questions, but it's still not there for everything that humans can do.

3. **Artificial super intelligence** – going beyond human ability to think in every aspect. It's not there yet, but it's possible that one day AI thinking will be better than most kinds of human thinking.

AI is *already* involved in lots of what we do in **modern life**. If you've ever had the next word you're typing suggested for you, browsed a 'For you' or 'Recommended' page, chatted with a bot or asked 'Hey Siri,' then you've engaged with programs designed to make interactions with computers seem more natural.

In the next couple of pages we'll check out some AI you've probably already used and take a look at how it all works so you can be ready for the **AI of the future**.

AI assistants

Siri is Apple's artificial intelligence **virtual assistant** – like Google Gemini, Amazon Alexa+, Microsoft Copilot and a bunch more – and can help you with a lot of things: making a call, getting directions, checking information, playing a song and so much more. It's like having an **incredibly knowledgeable butler** dedicated to helping you through your day.

When you ask, 'Hey Siri, what's the weather going to be tomorrow?' a lovely voice responds: 'Expect a partly sunny day with a top of 22 degrees.' While she *sounds* like she's coming from your phone, there's a lot more going on behind the screen.

What we call 'Siri' is a **computer program** installed on your phone that connects via the internet with **thousands of computers and servers** around the world.

If the Siri feature is enabled on an iPhone (or iPad, Apple Watch, HomePod etc.), it listens to every sound that you make 24 hours a day, 7 days a week. If it hears 'Hey Siri,' it **starts recording** what you're

> 'If you ask Siri or Alexa a normal question – like "What's your favourite colour?" – it comes back with a really weird answer. You can think you're talking to a real person, but it's just a program.'
> CHARLOTTE, 12

saying, then it sends that information via the internet to Apple's servers, where programs check what you said against a database of your own **speech patterns**, plus a *huge* library of human speech to figure out what you said.

If it did sound like 'Hey Siri' and then 'What's the weather going to be tomorrow?' the programs running on the computers around the world will use your **location information,** do an internet search for the forecast for tomorrow, summarise it briefly with AI and tell you what to expect.

It can be so helpful – and it can also feel **so human**! But as we're starting to engage more with AI, we need to remember that Siri (and other AI) is **not human**. It's the electrical circuits and disks inside your phone, the signals and wires carrying your information over the internet, and the electrical circuits and disks **processing your information** on other computers all around the world.

One day we might think of these electrical systems as something like **AI's 'brain'**, particularly as AI's capabilities surpass our own in various areas, but the differences to a biological human brain will remain.

'Computers are already the best game players, it's not surprising they can do everything else.'
GEORGE, 11

generative AI

First available to the public in 2022, **ChatGPT** is a computer program trained to answer questions in a natural way – just like a real-world knowledgeable expert would do – and it has **astonished** the world with its speed and clarity.

ChatGPT was the first widespread demonstration of what's known as **generative AI**, and there are now many examples of this technology being used in almost every area of life.

Generative AI works by first being trained on countless online examples of text, audio, images and videos made by humans. Imagine feeding a computer with every book, article, and piece of information it could possibly consume. Over time, it starts to build up a **database of patterns** in language, audio, video – everything it is trained on. It can then use this database of patterns and connections to predict what answers could be.

For instance, if you asked ChatGPT (or any other generative AI program) to write a story about a superhero, it would draw on all the superhero stories it has 'read' to fulfil your request. The AI doesn't actually **understand** the content like a human does, but it is incredibly good at **replicating** human writing and speaking styles based on the data it's been trained on. It's the same with any 'conversations' you might have with a chatbot.

People use generative AI to make heaps of things. I actually used it to write this book for me. (I'm **kidding**!) But AI can also 'create' images and video in any style you could imagine, write songs, transcribe content – and the list goes on!

We'll be using these capabilities more in the future in ways we've never even dreamed of, which is why it's helpful to understand a bit about how it all works.

The first thing to know is that generative AI doesn't always have what we'd call **commonsense** – the ability to understand and navigate the world without explicit instruction. The second is that what AI puts out *always* depends on **the rules** it was programmed with (i.e., *who* programmed it and *why*) and **the content** the program was trained on. Also, AI is increasingly being trained *on AI content*, meaning that over time there will be **less and less human input** in what we see.

AI can give us odd, laughable, wrong and **weird answers**, so we should take any information we get from AI with a grain of salt. With no commonsense, bias built into programming and AI being trained by AI, we should be careful about trusting anything it generates.

deepfakes

Deepfakes are computer-generated videos made to look like someone (or something) real. Just like video filters can put a cat's ears or a dog's nose on your face during a call, **deepfake technology** puts a filter on someone's whole face and even their voice to make it seem like someone else's: the prime minister, your school principal, your mum or even *you*.

Deepfakes are made using **deep learning** computer technology. This involves a computer program analysing specific situations over and over again until it gets really good at what it's doing – like adjusting images to look similar to source material.

There might be reasonable artistic, entertainment or public uses for deepfake technology, and some deepfakes can be funny. However, deepfakes can often be made **without consent** of the people involved, increasingly for disinformation, and they can even be a form of bullying. If there is a deepfake made of *you* without your consent, **tell a trusted adult** in your safety network.

The first deepfake went public in 2016, and the technology is already *so* much better. With a good program, trained for a long time, it's now nearly **impossible** to tell the difference between what's been generated by a camera or by deep-learning AI. This means *any* photo, video or speech recording we come across **could be fake**!

How can we trust any video we see? What happens if there's a video of a public figure doing something **immoral or illegal**? What if *they* claim it's a deepfake?

There aren't any **easy answers** to these questions. Images and videos can be more believable if you see the same thing from lots of different trusted sources, but it's tricky! It's not clear what deepfake capability will mean for how humans trust what they see in the future.

'Adults talk about being a doctor as like some sort of good job to aim for, but now they're saying computers could do it better.'

AMY, 14

THE FUTURE OF AI

Ever since the first sewing machine was invented, machines and computers have been getting **faster** and more **accurate** than humans at many jobs.

Toby Walsh, Professor of AI at the University of New South Wales, says that AI will likely end up doing a lot of the four Ds of work: the **dirty, dull, difficult and dangerous**. This sounds *great*!

But we do need to be careful. AI and AI-enabled robots will likely soon replace elements of many more jobs – lawyers, doctors, accountants, marketers, writers, designers ...

Most people think that AI won't ever really be able to replace *everything* that humans do, especially tasks that need human **emotional skills**, complex **decision-making** and **creativity**. So, jobs like being a comedian, bike mechanic, plumber or psychologist *should* be safe, but no-one really knows!

Technology has generally **created** more jobs than it destroys, but this mightn't always be the case in the future. What jobs might you want to do when you're older? Will AI or robots be doing them instead? What jobs will be left for humans? Can we even **imagine** them now?

Or maybe we won't need to work at all! When machines replaced some workers in factories during the

Industrial Revolution in the 1800s, one of the later consequences was the demand for better working conditions and more guaranteed time off work – to the point where an **8-hour working day** and a **2-day weekend** are now seen as normal. Maybe the AI Industrial Revolution will mean we'll all end up working 3-hour days with 5-day weekends. Sounds amazing!

But this future of kicking back and lazing around while machines do all the work for us while we still get paid a sweet wage isn't guaranteed. New technology has a curious way of always making the owners of that technology and the already rich **even richer**, but not necessarily improving the circumstances of other **people, communities or the environment** – especially in the short term.

Computers don't contribute to local communities. So, when a community's human workers are replaced with computers, those computers *may* be more **productive**, but they may also, in the long term, **undermine** the health of that community.

'It feels like computers and ChatGPT can do anything for you – like do all your homework, even go to university for you and get a degree ...'
THOMAS, 12

SO, WHAT NOW?

There are no easy answers and things are moving fast, but no matter what, it'll take some **deep human thinking and cooperation** to make a future where AI works in humanity's interests.

One thing's for certain: machines can do a lot and will continue to become more and more capable in the future.

Here's ChatGPT's #1 tip in response to this question: 'How should humans navigate a world with AI?'

> *Educate yourself about AI: The more you know about AI, the better equipped you will be to navigate a world with it. Make an effort to learn about the latest developments in AI technology, as well as the potential risks and benefits of AI.*

This sounds pretty reasonable – even if (and actually because) it's based on the vast amount of **material already published** by humans who have asked similar questions. ChatGPT's other recommendations include 'be cautious and skeptical, understand AI's limitations and embrace its potential'.

chapter 10

WHO'S WATCHING?

As you know, the average person with a smart phone – who occasionally shops online, uses Google Maps to navigate and has the usual bunch of social media accounts – gives away *enormous* amounts of **personal data** every day.

Sometimes **we don't care** if someone else sees what we're doing online (say, if we've searched for a cake recipe), but sometimes **we do care** (for example, if we want to keep our home address private).

What does all this mean for you? What can you do to maintain **privacy** on the internet, and what does that mean for **eSafety and transparency**?

'If you're on Google, and you type something in, or there's a site you usually go to, it saves! It learns.'
OLIVE, 12

YOUR DATA

Until reasonably recently, no-one knew who you chatted with, watched where you went, saw all your library searches or kept track of what you bought. But now all of this information is *almost always* **recorded online** somewhere, and *almost always* **connected to you** through your data and metadata. Google, Microsoft, Meta, Apple, Amazon and many other companies make a *lot* of money from selling your data to advertisers, and more than **95% of all English websites** run Google Ads services.

Once data is online, it can be very hard (often impossible) to erase at a later date. But what if you've posted something that you now don't want online, like a photo in fancy dress, a funny dance routine or a political opinion you've since rethought? Can you **get it taken down**? Most often the answer is no (more about this in Chapter 11).

While it *doesn't* mean you shouldn't go to fancy dress parties or dance stupidly or express any political opinions, it *does* mean you should **be careful** about what you post about yourself and others online – and what they post about you.

security, freedom, transparency and privacy

There are always trade-offs between **privacy and security**, and **secrecy and transparency**. Too much secrecy can make it easier for **illegal** things to happen. Too much surveillance can restrict our **freedom** to communicate or live our lives the way we want.

Governments have an important role in keeping us safe, and they collect information to help with this – both online and offline. Speed cameras help make sure cars don't go too fast. There are restrictions on the sale of dangerous materials. Police keep tabs on hurtful or illegal activity.

But the internet lets us be watched in a very different way to before. Governments around the world now engage in what's called **bulk surveillance** – where most of the data and metadata you generate is collected by most of the services and devices you use and stored *in bulk* for later analysis if needed.

It's not clear that we signed up for this – or where it might lead. Should we allow street cameras everywhere so governments can make sure no-one is breaking the law? What about in our homes? Should we allow Google Maps to share our car speeds with the police to automatically issue speeding fines?

Sometimes people say, 'If you don't do anything wrong, you should have nothing to hide.' But this makes a world where **no-one** is able to hide **anything**. And what's the impact of feeling *watched* all the time? It *might* be okay if you trust your government and agree with all of its laws, but what if you only agree with some? And what if a country's government doesn't act in its citizens' interests? Should it be okay for protesters to be surveilled? Or police officers? Or journalists? Or judges? Or politicians?

It's curious that as companies and governments get **more access** to our data, the less we can access information about **what they do**. Want to know who Google has sold your information to? Impossible! Want to know how Instagram classifies your personality? No chance. Want to know how many times the government has collected your data without your consent? You're dreaming.

BLOWING THE WHISTLE

There are real reasons why some information shouldn't be public, but there are also times when secrecy hides wrongdoings. In these cases, the world relies on the courage of whistleblowers – people within an organisation who expose wrongdoing: something secret, corrupt or illegal – and journalists to get the information out into the public, often at great personal cost.

Frances Haugen from Facebook, Tristan Harris from Google and Edward Snowden are three whistleblowers who let others know about unethical activities of the world's biggest tech companies. Chelsea Manning and Julian Assange exposed wrongdoings by governments going to war.

the trade-offs

It isn't always clear who should control what information is visible and what isn't, or what the trade-off between surveillance and freedom should be.

These are issues we should decide all together, but perhaps the maxim of the Cypherpunks (a movement started in the very early days of the internet) could be a helpful guide: 'privacy for the weak, transparency for the powerful'.

The Australian Government isn't allowed to spy on Australian citizens' data. *But* Australia is part of the **Five Eyes intelligence alliance**, and as part of that agreement the US, New Zealand, the UK and Canada *are* allowed to spy on Australian citizens (or anyone else) and then share that data with the Australian Government! Wild!

Other nations around the world, including countries in Asia and the European Union, have their own **intelligence gathering** and **sharing agreements**.

TIPS FOR PRIVACY AND SECURITY

There are plenty of reasons why you might want to **maintain privacy online**: to keep your home address, phone number and health information private, for example, or even just to share things with some people but not others.

As you know, the **default settings** on apps and websites are designed to gather (and share) as much information about you as possible. The thing is, unless you want to communicate only via carrier pigeon, pay exclusively in cash, navigate with a physical map and compass, and wear an invisibility cloak, it's nearly **impossible** to avoid having your data and metadata be

'My aunty made a Facebook page for me when I was little, and there are photos on there of me from ages ago that I can't even take down.'
STELLA, 12

collected, organised and monetised by companies and governments. However, there are some things you can do to keep your personal information **secure** and **avoid being tracked** so much.

consider some alternatives

The first thing is to recognise when you're giving away information online. (Reading this book is a good place to start!) Remember, the 'price' of Google, Instagram and most other 'free' services and platforms is usually your data. You often can **reduce tracking** on these services but not eliminate it.

There are also some **free non-tracking alternatives** for many services. For example:

- **DuckDuckGo** (duckduckgo.com) is a great alternative to Google that doesn't track your searches nor save your data.
- Unlike WhatsApp, which is owned by Meta and collects and sells your metadata, the messaging app **Signal** is open-source and doesn't collect your information.
- **Organic Maps** (organicmaps.app), which is open-source and based on OpenStreetMap, is a good swap for Google Maps.

- The **Firefox** internet browser is a commonly used non-tracking alternative to Chrome and Safari, which track you even when you're browsing 'privately'.

These are just a few suggestions, but a good guide is to look for alternatives produced by **open-source projects** and apps that use **end-to-end encryption**.

open-source software

Open-source software is free, volunteer-based and donation funded. The actual programming code itself can be **viewed and edited by anyone** as long as they keep it free for other people to use too. Open-source software helps keep the internet free – without having to pay for services with your data.

Without the billions of dollars of revenue that **surveillance-targeted advertising** provides, open-source alternatives aren't always as slick, but they do a pretty good job. There are great open-source alternatives for most computer programs. **Mozilla**, for example, produces the Firefox browser and Thunderbird mail client, and both contain software designed not to track or store your data.

PASSWORDS

Choosing passwords is an important part of online security. It can help protect your identity and private information and help you to avoid being **hacked**.

To avoid having to remember a squillion logins (or the same password for everything, which is not a good idea), you can use a **password manager** to store usernames and passwords in a secure password **vault** that only you have access to. Many web browsers (like Firefox and Chrome) have this built in, and there are also premium programs that provide a paid service for more security. You'll still need to come up with a good, strong, hard-to-crack password to protect that vault. That means 'password123' is out. So, what makes a good, strong, hard-to-crack password?

The **Electronic Frontier Foundation** has a game you can play to make up a strong pass*phrase*. Check it out at **eff.org/dice**, but basically you roll some dice, then match up the numbers you roll with six random words on their word lists. Combining these makes a **passphrase** *much* stronger than a short password – that you can then use to access your password vault.

JalapenoMollusc1472SnorkelGladiatorGreetingFan is an example master passphrase with a length and complexity that would help protect you against almost all **brute-force hacking** attempts (like a computer running for 8 hours checking different combos).

encryption

Encryption – which is built in to some, but not all, software – is a way of **scrambling** a message, and data more generally, so that only you and the intended reader can read it, and so that its contents can't be stored for later use. Encryption uses passwords and algorithms to **encode information**, and it can be a powerful way to keep your personal data and communications secure.

If you **encrypt** the message 'encryption is powerful' with the algorithm 'change every letter of the message to the one following it in the alphabet', you get the scrambled 'dmbqxoshnm hr onvdqetk'. Though it's **unreadable** at first glance, it's not *too* hard to crack – especially for a computer.

Modern encryption uses algorithms that mix up the message in a **very complex way** with a password that you provide. Encrypting 'encryption is powerful' with the password 'a_(totally_unguessable)_password' and the **Advanced Encryption Standard** (the encryption algorithm

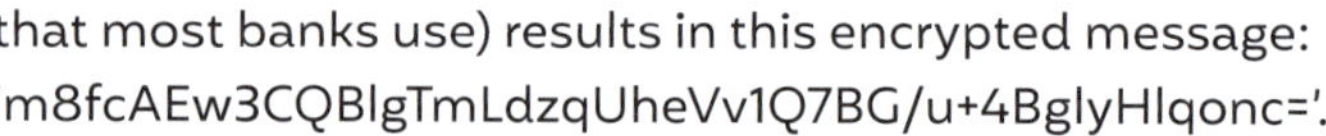

that most banks use) results in this encrypted message: 'm8fcAEw3CQBlgTmLdzqUheVv1Q7BG/u+4BglyHlqonc='.

This is *really* hard to turn back into the unencrypted message without knowing the password, even for the **most powerful computers** in the world. It's an example of what helps keep modern communications secure.

when there's no alternative

Sometimes there are **no good alternatives** available that don't track you or your data – like some of the Google Workspace, streaming services and social media. Ultimately, you (and your parents or carers) have to decide if and when it's okay to use these platforms and services.

If you *do* choose to use them, you can **reduce** how much you're being tracked by:

- **signing out of services and websites** (for example, if you're signed into Gmail, Google can track your activity across the internet)
- **switching off apps** when you're not using them (including adjusting their settings to not 'run in the background')
- **blocking email tracking** where available
- **turning off location tracking** on your device and in app settings
- **not allowing voice recording.**

You can also choose to use an **ad blocker**. Almost all internet browsers can have an add-on installed to block ads. Most of these ad blockers, such as **Adblock Plus** and **Privacy Badger**, have settings that allow you to decide what kinds of ads get blocked and on which sites. Since much content on the net is funded by advertising, these settings can help you to avoid invasive, distracting or unwanted content while still supporting sites with appropriate advertising.

And, as funny as it sounds, **paying** for a service (with your parents' consent) can also help with your privacy. Paying for **YouTube Premium** or **Spotify Premium**, for example, means you see and hear way *less* ads. It also means you have greater control on what content gets suggested for you. Your data will likely still be tracked, but getting more control over the advertising you see can help you have a healthier experience online.

'There should be restrictions on the internet for what young people can see.'
REUBEN, 11

advanced privacy

Beyond the standard tools that help maintain privacy online, there are **additional tools and techniques** that can hide your activity.

One way is through **virtual private networks** (VPNs), which change your IP address by moving it to another location (or even country) and encrypting the **web traffic**. This means you can access websites as if you were in a different country, and also that your internet or mobile service provider can't see what websites you visit. VPNs typically cost money to use, but are used a lot by people in different countries to go around **firewalls**, which block certain websites, games or apps. Many government organisations use VPNs to support secure communications and data handling.

Tor (standing for **The Onion Router**) is an open-source browser that uses multiple VPN-like layers (like an onion) to bounce information through so many different IP addresses that it becomes almost impossible to track where information is being sent or received from. Tor allows access to websites that aren't available through regular browsers (including the dark web).

The **Electronic Frontier Foundation** (eff.org) has more information on additional privacy techniques that could be used by journalists or whistleblowers wanting to avoid detection.

NOTE OF CAUTION

It's important here to be honest. Technology can be both helpful and harmful, and any tech that supports privacy can also hide or support illegal and unsafe behaviour, or expose users to potentially harmful and illegal content and websites – including what's known as the dark web.

Some level of visibility, tracking and monitoring can help us avoid dangerous content, protect us from unhealthy digital engagement or flag unsafe situations.

Adults, particularly those in a kid's safety network, should be aware that existence and use of any of these advanced privacy programs likely indicates something is being hidden.

chapter 11

THE FUTURE INTERNET

The internet is still very young, and it's changing faster than almost anything in human history. AI, augmented reality and body-web interfaces are already here, and things **beyond our imagination** are just around the corner. With technology moving so quickly, the **principles and ethics** underpinning *how* we interact with the internet need to be thought about too. And you get to **have a say** in that.

DIFFERENT PATHS FOR THE FUTURE

Decisions are being made today about many aspects of the internet. While the laws and technologies might seem technical, the ideas behind them are **simple** – and they should be decided all together.

Here are some of the questions being debated today:

- Should **deepfakes** need a disclaimer, and should they be allowed for **political advertising**?
- Who should be **responsible** for verifying a **user's age** – website owners, apps like Instagram, device-makers like Apple or a child's legal guardian?
- Should Australia's **eSafety Commissioner** be able to instruct Facebook or X to take down **violent** videos?
- Should companies be **allowed to charge** for AI content that was developed from **human-made** content?

What do **you** think?

Much of the early internet was built by volunteers with principles of **freedom of access, equality of data and openness** baked into the structure. Whether the internet of the future maintains these principles of goodwill is an open question.

The internet is growing by hundreds of millions of terabytes of data every day. All this information is stored physically in data centres all around the world. These need electricity to power them and even more electricity (and water) to keep them cool. Globally, the electricity consumption of data centres is now more than all of Australia – that's a lot!

The use of data is accelerating as we use the internet for more things. Generative AI and cryptomining, for example, use exponentially more data and computing power than visiting a traditional static website – and the technologies of the future will likely require even more.

The manufacturing of the devices we use to access the internet has environmental impacts too. The metals, rare earth minerals, plastics and glass used in devices all need to be mined or produced somewhere. If these aren't mined responsibly, people, animals and the environment can all suffer.

And to add to that: e-waste is being generated globally 5 times faster than it's being recycled. You can take steps to help by recycling your e-waste (public libraries can often take it, or know where you should go), buying responsibly, and building your awareness about the broader environmental impacts of how the economy works.

change is possible

Two hundred years ago, the weekend didn't exist! Heaps of people (including kids) were forced to work 12 hours a day, 6 days a week, with **terrible pay and minimal protections** for safety. People could also dump rubbish in the ocean, spill chemicals in a creek and be jailed for their sexuality or religion.

Today, *thankfully*, the world – well, much of the world – is different. Now, many people can work just 4 days a week if they want, kids under 15 aren't forced to work dangerous jobs, the environment is better protected and there is much greater acceptance of diversity.

All this is to say that **change is possible**. It's not always quick but, if enough people get together and want to change something, it can and *does* happen.

It sometimes feels like the internet is a **global space** that doesn't have to answer to any country's laws (something internet companies often want to be the case). But the law can and does apply to what happens online. And **new laws** can be made to change what happens on the net.

Here are some **good news stories** – and there are more every year!

The right to be forgotten

In 2014, a Spanish man found old news articles on Google reporting that he owed people money. As he'd long since paid his debts, he asked Google to take down the articles and the **European Court of Justice** ruled they had to do just that. As a result, European citizens now have the **right to be forgotten** and request information about them to be taken down, de-linked and deleted!

'Online Eraser'

Community activists in California successfully advocated in 2015 for an **Online Eraser law**, which allows anyone **under the age of 18** to be able to remove almost any information they have shared online.

'I don't want all of my photos to be able to be seen by anyone forever.'
CLARE, 14

If a Californian wants to **delete** an embarrassing photo of their younger self at a costume party, or a baby photo of them playing under a sprinkler, they can.

eSafety support

In 2021, Australia became the **first country in the world** to appoint an eSafety Commissioner to keep its citizens safer online. And they're doing a great job – the eSafety.gov.au website is a valuable resource for people all over the world.

Health

In 2019, South Korea became one of the first countries to recognise **internet addiction** as a formal mental health disorder. They've established **Centres for Youth Internet Addiction Treatment** across the country that have helped young people with addictions to gaming, social media, online shopping and much more.

Net neutrality

The principle of net neutrality – treating all data **equally** through telecommunication networks – has now been enshrined in many countries across the world including India, Brazil, Japan and Canada (but not Australia – yet!), meaning that no-one can pay for **privileged or priority access** through data servers.

things you can do

Change really is possible. The steps you just read about have made the internet a safer, freer and more equal space, and have helped our interactions with it be healthier and happier. Many more steps can be taken if we'd like.

What **future internet** do you want to see? How can you help to make it?

Here are some suggestions:

- Talk with your friends, parents and school about **the digital world you want to live in**, what should and shouldn't be private, and work together to make it happen.
- If you see something happening online that's wrong, you can **be an upstander not a bystander** by calling it out or giving it a thumbs-down if you're comfortable.
- Ask your school to give you **non-tech options** for your work where possible.
- Have a chat with your teachers about what you'd like them to do **without any technology** – see if they'd like to take part in Offtober or TechFreeTuesdays (see **offtober.org**).

'When I have my phone, I don't have to worry about anything – I can get in contact with people or find out anything if I need to.'
HARRIET, 11

- If you find yourself writing code, **code with conscience**. Be aware of how algorithms can influence or prejudice people and **invent things with safety-by-design**.
- If you have ideas on how to make the internet better, **write to the eSafety Commissioner or your local member of parliament**. There are a lot of people concerned about your education and wellbeing, and they have a responsibility to make sure you're heard.
- As you get closer to voting age, check out or become involved with the political parties that are advocating for **the future that you want to see**.
- Check out **behindthescreens.me** for further reading suggestions.

You'll be coming up with your own ideas too!

GOING FORWARD

Humans are **social** beings! More than any animal in the history of the world, we love to communicate, share information, stay in touch and do things together.

The internet lets this happen on a scale, and at speeds, previously **unimaginable**. Smartphones, computers, AI and the internet are some of the most **incredible inventions** of humankind. They – and so many other digital technologies yet to be invented – are changing our lives at an **amazing pace**.

You're in the driver's seat for how to engage with it all. It'll take some **experimentation**, but you're going to figure it out. You know what **makes you feel good** and what doesn't.

It's not all roses and puppies on the internet, and there are people and companies online that are trying to get you to spend money and do things that aren't in your **best interest**. But it's not all negative or dishonest, either. You're going to be the expert on what feels rewarding and worthwhile – as well as what doesn't feel quite right. The law and your safety network are there to help too.

How you're going to engage with the internet is **beyond the imagination** of any adult today – including me! But I hope that this book will **help** you on your way.

—Nij
Naarm, Australia
behindthescreens.me

FURTHER READING

A full reference list is available at **behindthescreens.me**, but here are some websites for you to visit if you're interested in further reading:

- eSafety.gov.au
- kidshelpline.com.au
- headspace.org.au
- gamequitters.com
- offtober.org
- families.google
- apple.com/au/families
- familycenter.meta.com/au
- bullyingnoway.gov.au
- au.reachout.com
- eff.org

ACKNOWLEDGEMENTS

Aly O'Brien, thanks heaps for thinking this book was a good idea from the start. Thanks to UQP for bringing it to life: Lauren Mitchell for the kind yet razor-sharp contemporary editing and Cathy Vallance for the calm, sure-footed guidance to cross the finish line. Aśka for channelling your orthogonal brilliance in visual storytelling to all the thorny ideas. Australia's eSafety Commissioner Julie Inman Grant, headspace CEO Jason Trethowan, psychologist Jocelyn Brewer, Professor Amanda Third, and YouTube's Head of Trust & Safety Machine Learning Dr Seiji Armstrong all provided generous, authoritative, cutting-edge perspectives on the online world for young people – thank you. Thanks also to Todd Sampson and Dr Norman Swan – both leading voices in the conversation about healthy tech interaction – for your kind and generous support of this book. To the kids at Footscray West Primary, Yarraville Primary, Princes Hill and The Gap State High (most names have been changed) – in particular Jay and Maddy – thanks for your honest insights. The kids are going to be alright. Finally, to Sally for making everything better and for having all the ideas that I later claim as my own.

ABOUT THE AUTHOR AND ILLUSTRATOR

Dr Niraj (Nij) Lal is an ANU Visiting Fellow and host of the ABC's *Imagine This* kids' podcast, and he's passionate about making science work in society's interests. He has a PhD in physics from the University of Cambridge, has appeared on *Play School* and *Catalyst*, and his awards include the 2021 Celestino Eureka Prize for Promoting Understanding of Science and the 2022 Royal Societies of Australia and New Zealand Piasecki Prize for Outstanding Writing on Social Change. He lives in Melbourne with his partner Sally and their three kids.

Aśka (pronounced *Ash-ka*) is creative dynamite, an award-winning graphic novelist, an ex-quantum physicist, and a hugely engaging and popular presenter. Having published more than a dozen books and comics, Aśka is passionate about visual literacy and teaching people how to 'write with pictures'. Watch out for her latest release, a YA graphic novel titled *The Friendship Paradox* (Allen & Unwin) – a mix of a physics road trip and a story about figuring out how to make friends. Fun fact: despite being a fan of technology, Aśka has never owned a smart phone. She thinks everyone should read this book!